National T[rust]
Harting D[owns]

Take in spectacular views, then descend into secluded valleys to discover fascinating wildlife – and the darkest place on the downs

Welcome to Harting Down

Look to the hills
Pause a while to take in the stunning panorama from the car park. Stretching out in front of you is the flat plain of the Weald. The ridge on the horizon is the Hog's Back, with the North Downs beyond.

☞ *Walk up hill from car park, through gate, then up higher track to top of Harting Hill.*

The war effort
Notice the two tracks running parallel up the hill. The higher one is the original South Downs Way; the lower is where the path was re-routed during World War Two to make way for a potato crop.

☞ *Go over brow of hill and straight down.*

Ancient markers
The strange parallel mounds at the bottom of the hill are known as the 'cross ridge dykes'. They date back to the Iron Age, and would probably have had wooden fences on top. It is thought that they could have been a 'check-point' on the transport route across the ridgeway, or boundary markers.

☞ *Follow right-hand track up hill other side, keeping hedge to your left.*

Watch where you walk
Incredibly, one square metre of the grassland below your feet could support 30-40 plant species. Many butterflies and insects rely on these downland plants. For example, bird's-foot trefoil, with its bright yellow flowers, feeds the caterpillars of the common blue butterfly.

☞ *Just over top of the hill, turn left and go through gate.*

A whiff of alcohol
If gin and tonic comes to mind as you descend the hill, it's not wishful thinking! The evergreen bushes all around you are junipers – this is one of the best sites for them in the south. Their fragrant black berries are used to flavour gin. In spring, the ground is carpeted with buttery-yellow cowslips, a common ingredient in potent country wines.

juniper

☞ *Go through gate at bottom and across valley.*

Iron Age hill fort
Rising in front of you is Beacon Hill, the site of an Iron Age hill fort. Its ramparts now appear as a ridge enclosing the field on the summit. This fort was probably built as an animal enclosure and symbol of power, rather than for defence (see Cissbury Ring leaflet).

☞ *Take diagonal track to right at base of Beacon Hill (not through centre of valley). Or extend your walk to top of Beacon Hill (see map for directions).*

BEACON HILL TELEGRAPH

The concrete foundations on the hilltop are the remains of a telegraph station. It was one of a series created in the late 1700s to give warning of French invasion. Shutters on the roof could be opened and closed in sequence to pass messages from Portsmouth Docks to London, the whole process taking just fifteen minutes. After 1814, telegraph lines were replaced by the new semaphore system.

☞ *Turn right at blue waymarking sign (from here you can see views to the Isle of Wight) and follow track to bottom of hill.*

ANTS AND BUTTERFLIES

Down the hill, the ground erupts into countless anthills, housing colonies of yellow meadow ants. The anthills work like storage heaters, building up heat from the sun to keep the colony warm. Touch them gently to feel the warmth. Common blue butterflies have a fascinating relationship with these ants. A sugary secretion from their caterpillars encourages the ants to 'milk' them. In return, the ants care for the caterpillars until they pupate.

POND LIFE

The dew pond in the valley bottom was re-created in 1990, on the site of a former 17th century pond. It is one of three on Harting Down. Traditionally, such ponds supplied water for grazing animals, relying on collecting rain water not dew. No longer needed for sheep, this pond is a haven for wildlife such as frogs and dragonflies.

☞ *At junction of tracks in valley bottom, take path straight ahead from the hill you have just descended, and go through barrier into yew wood. (If you visit again, try the alternative return route marked on the map which takes you through an old beech wood.)*

The darkest place

Even on the hottest day, the yew wood is cold and dark. Some of the trees are up to 300 years old. Yew is said to ward off evil spirits, hence it is often seen in churchyards. Its elastic branches were traditionally used to make bows. Note the lack of vegetation under the trees – light cannot penetrate, so few plants survive. Yews are favourite nesting sites for birds like robins, wrens, thrushes and finches.

☞ At top of hill, follow path round to right and through barrier. Turn right at finger post by large beech tree. At end of track, go through opening to right (not gate). Follow grassy path which leads over brow of hill then back down to car park.

Countryside Kids

Wildlife talent show

🙂 A rare and magical sight on the down is adders 'dancing'. This is really two males wrestling for territory – they rear up and sway in an attempt to push their opponent to the ground.

🙂 Don't laugh too loud when you pass the hill called 'Granny's Bottom'. If you are quiet, you might spot some fallow deer. In October, the bucks put on a show for the does, thrashing at trees (and other males) with their antlers, and making deep belching noises. This is called the 'rut'.

🙂 Granny's Bottom is also the place to hear nature's most famous singer – the nightingale – on many summer afternoons and evenings.

A common question

Harting Down is a registered common, and is also designated as a Local Nature Reserve for its valuable chalk grassland. The grassland owes its diversity of wildlife to the tradition of grazing. Commoners currently exercise rights to graze the down. Commoning is a remnant of the Medieval manorial system – the lord of the manor owned the land, but residents (commoners) had legal rights to help them make a living. The lord was not allowed to carry out any act which would deny these rights.

☞ *About this walk...*

Distance: 2 miles (allow 1½ hours)

Terrain: Several hills. Muddy in places

Start: Harting Down car park (NT), off B2141, 5½ miles SE of Petersfield

Public Transport: For bus information Traveline on 0871 200 22 33 or visit www.traveline.org.uk

Facilities: None on walk. Nearest in South Harting or Uppark House (NT – for details call 01730 825857).

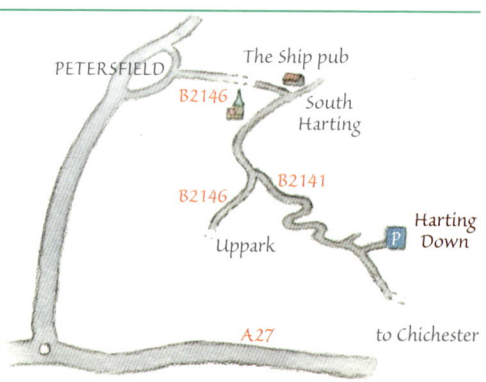

Welcome to Drovers

A famous sporting estate
Drovers has long been connected with country sports. Pheasant shooting still takes place from September to late January (usually Saturdays). You may be asked to wait briefly whilst a drive is being completed.

Honeycomb Copse

Cucumber Farm

☞ *Take path off A286 which leads over bridge and round cricket pitch. Go behind pavilion, then across three stiles. Follow the sunken track up hill.*

A tangle of trees
The hedgerow along the track is a weave of hawthorn, ash, hazel, oak and dogwood. The wealth of species indicates that it is very old.

cricket pitch

☞ *Cross bridge, then go sharp right and up to stile.*

By rail to the races
The bridge crosses a disused railway, once part of the Chichester to Midhurst line. This was opened in 1881 and closed to passengers in 1935. Singleton Station nearby was built to be large enough to cope with the crowds of visitors to Goodwood Racecourse.

Weald & Downland Museum car park

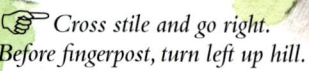
hazel coppice — bus stops — A 286

☞ *Cross stile and go right. Before fingerpost, turn left up hill.*

A riot of colour
In summer, the hillside is speckled with the yellow, blue and pink of cowslips, harebells and common spotted orchids. The air is scented with wild thyme. Sheep and cattle grazing is crucial here to preserve the turf and its wildlife.

☞ *Pause before brow to look back at views.*

Valley panorama
In the valley to your left is Cucumber Farm which dates back to the 1700s. The name is thought to derive from 'cow-combe', relating to its use as a dairy farm. On the horizon to the right you can see the gleaming white stands of Goodwood race course.

☞ *Follow path into wood.*

Ancient beeches
In the dappled shade of Honeycomb Copse, you can find many ancient, gnarled beech trees, some planted in the 1800s to commemorate the Battle of Trafalgar. The bramble-covered fallen trees support valuable communities of beetles.

☞ *Cross the open grassy area, go through stile, then straight on round field edge to next gate.*

Medieval deer park
This area was once the centre of an extensive deer park, recorded as being owned by the Earl of Arundel in 1327.

bus stop

START

Its lodge was located in the fields to your left – archaeologists have found many oyster shells, no doubt the remains of great banquets held there.

👉 Turn right and walk past the buildings, then go right again. At hedge, veer off to left and follow path across arable field. At other side, go over stile into wood. At junction, go left and follow path to next junction. Go right, then immediately left up path.

WHAT IS COPPICING?

Look out for coppiced hazel trees here. Coppicing is the traditional practice of cutting trees back to the stumps, so that numerous new shoots grow. These shoots are used for making fencing and thatching spars. To minimise disturbance to the ground, the timber here is extracted by heavy horses from the Weald and Downland Museum. Coppicing benefits many wildflowers, as well as the rare dormouse.

👉 At next junction go right then straight over crossroad and down to main road. (Bus stops located here). Cross road and follow track on other side. After about 100 metres, take first track to left which goes around a field. In the wood, take first track off to right. At top of steep rise, (after about 70 metres) go left.

AUTUMN COLOURS

Don't miss a walk here in autumn when the wood is aflame with orange, yellow and red.

👉 At next junction, turn right and follow to next junction. Turn left and walk to top of hill, then stay on main path which goes down to left through beech wood.

BLUEBELL CASCADE

As you walk down this path in April, you will be greeted by a stunning cascade of bluebells on the other side of the valley.

👉 At next junction, turn right and follow track round, up steep hill and down other side.

BUTCHER'S BROOM

As you descend, look out for the spiny evergreen shrub, butcher's broom, amidst the holly. In the past this was used by butchers to clean their chopping blocks – feel it and you'll know why.

👉 Follow path round to left and by meadows. Go through farm gates and take steep path to left. Go up field, through small gate at top, then left. After about 75 metres, take path on right. Cross stile then go straight up hill along the field edge. About half way up, go through gate on left. Follow path (can be slippery) and over next stile.

NATURE RESERVE

You now cross Levin Down Nature Reserve, owned by the Goodwood Estate, and leased to the Sussex Wildlife trust. See information panel by the stile.

👉 Keep on path, over several stiles, then down steps and field and onto the road. Go left, then right at crossroad. (For Fox Goes Free pub, go straight on at crossroad.)

(note: map not to scale)

☞ *Take footpath on right across arable field. At far side, follow path to right, cross road and walk on right-hand pavement with leads under a tiled roof. Continue past church, through gate, then right onto lane. Go left at road. At main road, go left and back to start.*

Countryside Kids

TARZAN SWINGS AND NOISY THINGS!

😊 See if you can spot the shrub called old man's beard, which covers the hedges in autumn with white feathery fruits. Its long stems dangle over the bushes like Tarzan swings.

😊 Fallow deer live here, but they are shy and will hide from you. Scan the ground for their hoof prints. Each hoof is divided into two (called cloven).

😊 Listen for the loud 'kok-kok-kok' cry of pheasants in the woods. One might dash past you in a flurry of russet and green. Look out for their food hoppers by the paths.

☞ *About this walk…*

DISTANCE: 4 miles (allow 3½ hours). Possible short cut by catching bus where walk crosses A286 (see map)

TERRAIN: Strenuous walk with steep climbs, numerous stiles and muddy tracks

START: Cricket pitch in Singleton, off A286 Chichester to Midhurst road, 5 miles N of Chichester. Bus stop opposite, or park at Weald & Downland Museum – car park open every day except Christmas Day (10.30am to 6pm summer/4pm winter), but busy during special events. For opening times call 01243 811348

PUBLIC TRANSPORT: For bus information call Traveline on 0871 200 22 33 or visit www.traveline.org.uk

FACILITIES: Fox Goes Free pub in Charlton. Pubs/tearooms in Singleton

PLEASE NOTE: *As the walk crosses mainly farmland, you are asked to keep dogs under close control at all times to avoid disturbance to animals. Please leave all gates as you find them.*

🌳 National Trust
Slindon Estate

Towering white tree trunks, ghostly reminders of the once magnificent beech wood, stand watch over the crowded wildlife below

Welcome to the Slindon Estate

Take middle track from car park. Turn left through first gate and follow track.

Floods of flowers
Don't miss a visit in May when a sea of bluebells washes over the woods. The scattered piles of branches, cut to allow the bluebells more light, make valuable wildlife habitats. In summer, look out for the shower of golden-yellow flowers on broom, and elegant purple foxgloves.

☞ *When you meet the grassy bank, veer right along main track.*

Ancient deer park
This bank is called the 'pale', and marks the boundary of the Medieval Slindon deer park. The bank would have had a ditch inside and a formidable fence on top to retain the fallow deer. The original manor house was sited near the present Slindon House, overlooking the deer park. If you look to the right you can see the house on the hilltop.

☞ *Follow track where it cuts through the pale, then go immediately right.*

The beech tombstones
The white tree trunks rising above the woodland are the remains of the once famous Slindon beeches (see back page). They may look lifeless, but inside each is a hive of activity. Birds such as woodpeckers, owls and kestrels nest high in the decaying stumps, along with colonies of bats and many insects.

☞ *Keep following main track as it veers right.*

Untidy woodland homes
When the tall beech trees fell, light flooded onto the ground encouraging dormant seeds to germinate. First to emerge were birch trees – you can see them all around, strewn with honeysuckle and brambles. This regeneration may look unruly, but it is rich in wildlife. Dormice make their nests from shredded honeysuckle bark, grass and leaves.

☞ *Detour a few metres behind large yew tree on left for a trip into the past.*

Slindon by Sea
Imagine you have stepped back in time some 500,000 years, when the sea level was 30 metres higher than today. *The bank you are standing on is a raised beach overlooking a steep-sided chalk cliff. At the cliff base, Early Stone Age people are collecting pebbles and flint to make tools....* Archaeological finds validate this picture of past life at Slindon.

☞ *Return to main track and continue.*

Ivy-clad trees
Notice the ivy on the trees to your right. Its nectar-rich flowers attract insects, while birds feed on the berries. The use of ivy at Christmas arose from a belief that it kept malicious goblins at bay. The surviving beech trees to your left are reminders of the past grandeur of the wood.

☞ *Follow track through pale again, then through gate. At junction, fork left.*

Fallen glory
The track passes a huge chalky mound on the left, the root system of a fallen lime tree. It provides a warm habitat for burrowing insects such as solitary wasps. Beside it is a curved wall, the remains of a grand summerhouse, built in the 1800s.

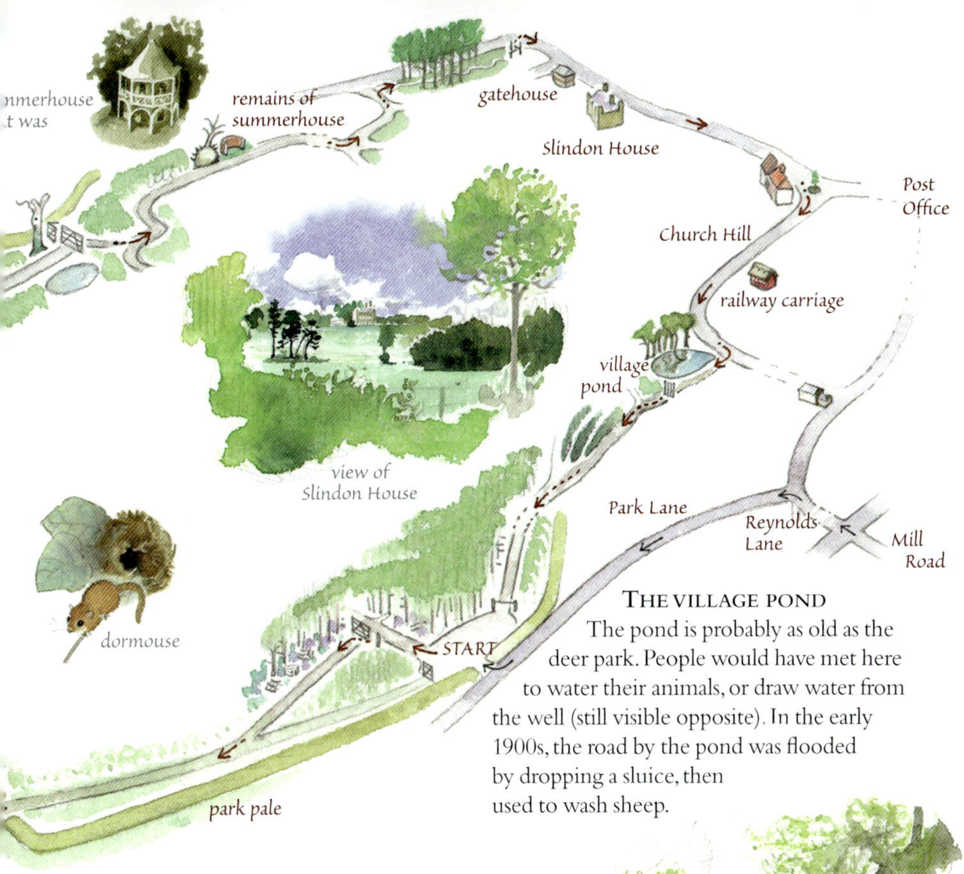

THE VILLAGE POND

The pond is probably as old as the deer park. People would have met here to water their animals, or draw water from the well (still visible opposite). In the early 1900s, the road by the pond was flooded by dropping a sluice, then used to wash sheep.

☞ *Follow track as it veers left to road. Turn right along path though trees, then right towards the village.*

SLINDON VILLAGE

You now pass the North gatehouse of Slindon House, let to Slindon College. The National Trust owns two-thirds of the village, most of its properties painted in the estate colour of burgundy.

☞ *Follow road until you meet Church Hill. Turn right.*

HISTORIC COTTAGES

Here you pass one of the oldest houses in Slindon, number 2 Church Hill, thought to be early 16th century. Note the galleting on the walls of number 11, where the mortar is decorated with pieces of flint. The thatched railway carriage on the left ran on London trains from 1874 until 1906. On the right, you pass The Grange, once the home of poets Madame Belloc and her son Hillaire.

☞ *Take path to the right on far side of pond, through gate, then left at fork.*

BACK TO THE WOODS

The cobbled path you follow was once a carriage drive. In winter, the drainage ditches on either side often form gurgling streams. On warm summer days, colourful butterflies dance and dart along the path, including speckled woods, red and white admirals, and brimstones.

☞ *Keep on main track which leads back to car park.*

Countryside Kids

NOISY, CREEPY AND SMELLY THINGS

☻ Listen for the rapid drumming sound of woodpeckers. Look out for the small circular nest holes they drill high in the trees.

☻ Can you guess why the mushroom called 'stinkhorn' is so-named? Take a whiff when they appear in August and you'll know!

☻ Dead wood provides food for many insects. Lift a piece and see what scurries away – then put it back so you don't leave them homeless.

The Great Storm

Slindon's magnificent beech trees were once highly prized, their seeds being sold worldwide. In October 1987, most of them were flattened by the Great Storm, which whirled through the woods like a tornado, wrenching out trees that had stood for up to 250 years. Most of the fallen trees were cleared and sold for timber. The dead wood left on the ground provides an important habitat for fungi and insects. These 'rotters' turn it into raw nutrients which are re-absorbed into the soil.

 About this walk…

DISTANCE: 2 miles (allow 1½ hours)

TERRAIN: Easy, flat walk. Pushchair accessible

START: Park Lane car park, Slindon, off A29, 6 miles N of Bognor Regis

PUBLIC TRANSPORT: Compass bus 84/5 stops at Frontwell. Short walk through A27 underpass

FACILITIES: The Spur Pub on the A29 at bottom of village

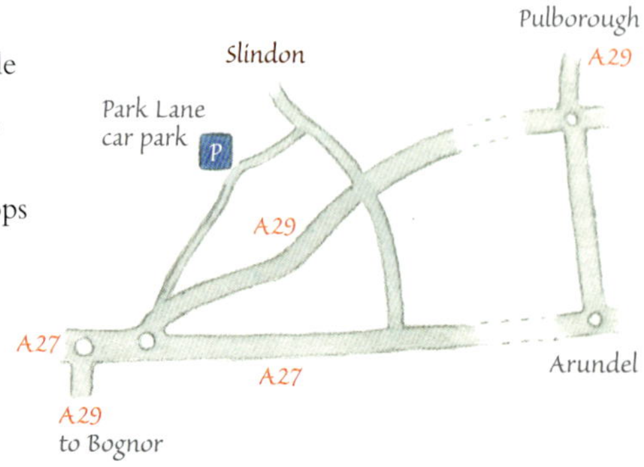

National Trust
Cissbury Ring

An ancient hill fort towering over the downs, its ramparts giving breathtaking views over patchwork fields to the sea

Welcome to Cissbury Ring

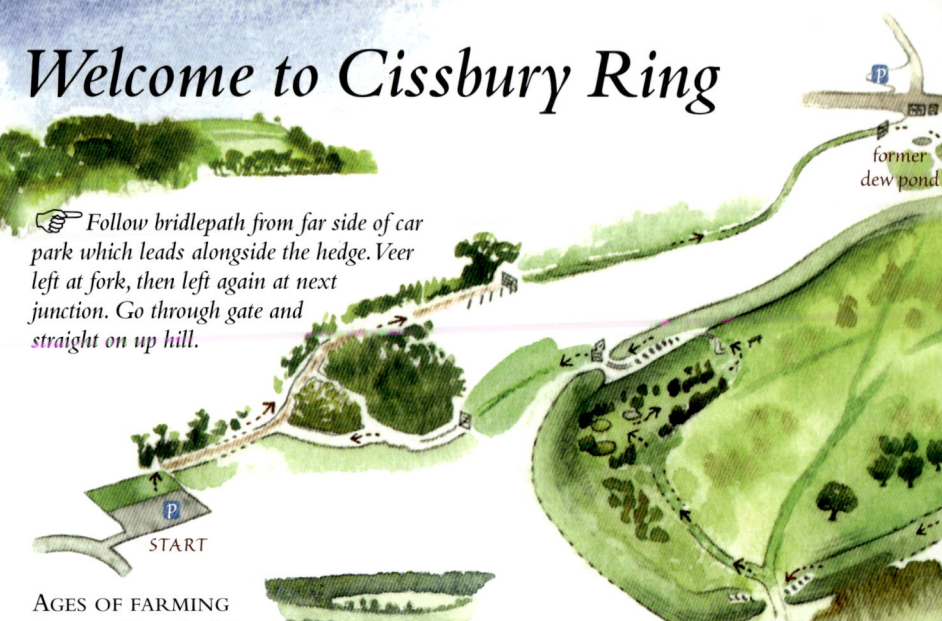

☞ *Follow bridlepath from far side of car park which leads alongside the hedge. Veer left at fork, then left again at next junction. Go through gate and straight on up hill.*

Ages of farming
As you walk up the hill, Cissbury Farm appears on the left, a sheep farm which has been worked by five generations of the same family (since 1810). The double-gabled farmhouse lies in the valley bottom. Notice the ridges in the fields, formed during the Iron Age by ploughing. In those days, people lived beside the fields, only sheltering in the hill fort in times of threat.

☞ *Go through next gate and pause by car park.*

whitethroat

Chain of hill forts
Cissbury Ring is one of a series of hill forts. You can see two of them from here – to your left are the trees of Chanctonbury Ring, while straight ahead is the Devil's Dyke (just past the aerials). Cissbury Ring is the second largest hill fort in the country, the largest being Maiden Castle in Dorset. For more details, look at the information panel in the car park.

Fairy story?
The often muddy hollow to the right of the car park was once a dew pond. Unbelievably, it still provides a home for fairy shrimps. These tiny, extremely rare creatures can lie dormant for years until the pond fills with water. Vulnerable to predators, they cannot survive in permanent ponds.

☞ *Facing Cissbury Ring, go left from car park and follow the lower bridlepath (blue waymark) which leads diagonally up the hill.*

Haven for birds
This sheltered track is the medieval route over the hill. In summer, it is lined with the pink and purple of rosebay willowherb. The shrubs and trees are important for migrating birds, including whitethroats, blackcaps and willow warblers, which find food and shelter here before and after their long journeys.

Orchid paradise
In summer, it is worth taking a slight detour into the area at the top of the bridlepath (to left of gate). It was bulldozed in the 1960s to deter rabbits, then left to re-colonise. From late May until July it is awash with colourful orchids including pyramidal, fragrant, early purple and common spotted.

☞ *Go through gate then straight on for a few metres. Then turn right and head for entrance of hill fort.*

Refuge in the fort
You now enter the impressive Iron Age hill fort, built by local people as a symbol of power and a refuge in times of threat. Originally the bank would have had a deep ditch in front and a timber fence on top, creating a formidable stronghold.

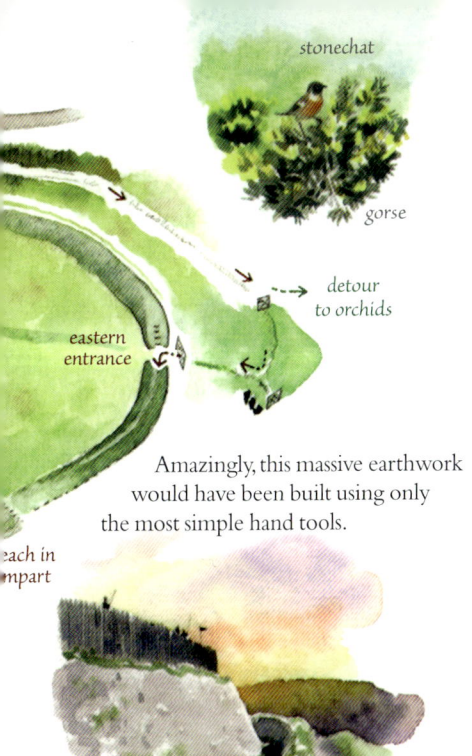

Amazingly, this massive earthwork would have been built using only the most simple hand tools.

☞ *Go down steps, turn right and take the small track which goes along the brow of the hill.*

Ever-useful gorse

The yellow of gorse brightens up the hilltop year-round. It is also a very useful shrub. In Saxon times it was called 'furze' and was used as firewood as it ignites easily and burns at a high temperature. The crushed foliage made a valuable winter feed for animals. Today it provides an endless larder for wildlife. Listen for stonechats perched on the higher branches, their calls sounding like stones being tapped together.

☞ *Before the path veers to the right, take a detour into the scrub ahead.*

Mining for flint

The strange hollows you come across are the remains of Stone Age flint mines (dating back 5-6,000 years). Over 270 pits have been found here. The flint was used to make tools, and there is evidence that it was exported as far away as the eastern Mediterranean. The shafts were over 12 metres deep, with many galleries radiating out from the base.

☞ *Go up steps on left of entrance and along the rampart. Pause at the breach.*

Centuries of defence

Overlooking 78 miles of coastline, this is an ideal site for defence. Archaeologists have found beach pebbles here, presumably hoarded as Iron Age sling shots. The hill was also an Armada beacon site. The breach you cross in the rampart was made during the Second World War to make way for a 100lb gun, which was fired from here to ships at sea. An anti-aircraft gun was sited in the hollow beside the breach.

☞ *Return to path and continue to bench. Drop down hill and follow rampart to left. Take steps down on right, through kissing-gate and down track to gate. The path leads back to the car park.*

Protecting the Hill Fort

Around 50,000 people visit Cissbury Ring each year, their footsteps causing considerable erosion to the ramparts and paths. Groups of volunteers regularly help the Trust in the time-consuming task of restoring this damage.

It can take one week for 15 people to repair just 450 metres of the ramparts (the total length is just over a mile). To find out more about volunteering for the Trust please call 01243 814554.

For more information about the Iron Age and the archaeology of Cissbury Ring, visit Worthing Museum.

Countryside Kids

Battles with ships … and bugs!
☺ Stand on the Iron Age ramparts and imagine you are on the look-out for invading Roman ships? Can you see any ships at sea now?

☺ In the Second World War, a huge gun was dragged up the hill to fire at enemy ships at sea. How many miles away do you think the sea is from here? (*See below)

☺ You can see a rare plant called field fleawort near the flint mines. In the Stone Age, people put it in their beds to keep fleas and bugs away!

field fleawort

(*Answer – 3½ miles)

☞ *About this walk…*

Distance: 2 miles (allow 2 hours)

Terrain: Long gradual climb, steep descent, some steps

Start: Storrington Rise car park (signposted Cissbury Ring), Findon Valley, on A24, 3 miles N of Worthing

Public Transport: Bus stops on A24 (½ mile away). For bus information call Traveline on 0871 200 22 33 or visit www.traveline.org.uk

Facilities: None on walk. Nearest in Findon Valley

Welcome to Fulking Downs

Before you leave the crowds behind, get your bearings by looking at the viewpoint by the stone seat. Fulking Hill is to your left as you look over the scarp slope. Find out more about the Devil's Dyke, and alternative local walks, on our website – www.nationaltrust.org.uk

☞ Follow path to left, cross stile and go straight on, heading for cleft in grassy bank.

THE DOMAIN OF SHEEP
Sheep have been a constant feature on Fulking Downs for 4,000 years. Their grazing has resulted in the wildlife-rich grassland we see today. The grassy mounds you pass through form the ramparts of an Iron Age hill fort. When under attack, sheep and cattle may have been herded inside for safekeeping.

☞ After passing through the bank, walk along ridge, making for lower bridlegate ahead. Go through gate and down main track to right.

SHEEP ROADS
En route, you will suddenly come across deep hollows, known as bostals, which date back to Medieval times. They are tracks etched into the chalk by sheep being driven daily from their night-time pens on fallow fields, onto the downs. Notice the 'dual carriage-way' where two bostals run side by side.

☞ Cross bostals and continue on path. Where track forks by National Trust sign, go left. Or take a short detour down path to right to see the spring at the Shepherd & Dog pub.

SPRING-LINE VILLAGES
The spring is one of three which gush from this stretch of the downs. The villages of Fulking, Edburton and Poynings have developed around them. The springs are formed by water emerging where porous chalk meets waterproof clay near the bottom of the hill.

☞ Follow main track, forking left at junction, and cross stile. Continue. After going through a hollow, go left up path. Cross stile then turn right and take steps into bostal. Follow track down, taking left-hand bostal at fork.

hill dips here s gate is unseen before brow of coombe

head for post on outward journey

START

Note the tiny terraces on the hillside – these are tracks cut by sheep as they cross the slopes.

☞ *Before gate at top of hill, turn left and follow fence-line along ridge.*

HUMPS AND BUMPS
The curious mounds you cross are the Medieval remains of Edburton Castle. This is thought to have been a look-out post for nearby Bramber Castle.

☞ *Cross the mounds and go through right-hand stile. Walk down towards pylon on edge of ridge.*

RESTORING FLOWERY GRASSLAND
Over the last 50 years, 90 per cent of chalk grassland in Britain has been ploughed up. The field you are crossing had met a similar fate until coming under the care of the Trust in 1987. It has since been restored to grass. In time, flowers such as cowslips, orchids and wild thyme will again knit brilliant colours into the turf.

cowslip

☞ *Go through wooden gate and take narrow path which goes up hill (to left of main track).*

TWO SIDES TO A STORY
Take a closer look at the sides of the bostal. On your left is the sunny south-facing slope, sprinkled with grassland flowers. In June, wild thyme steals the show with its mauve flowers and delicate scent. The damper, north-facing slope supports bright green mosses, enlivening the weary winter grassland.

☞ *Go through gate and along ridge track.*

HOLE IN THE WALL
Near the bottom of the bostal, look left to see a wall with a hole in the base. This is a Victorian lime kiln, recently restored by the Trust. The information panel will tell you more about it.

detour to pub   Shepherd & Dog

☞ *Turn left before five-barred gate, and follow path over two stiles. Skirt foot of hill until you reach waymark post. Follow bostal up hill.*

TAKES YOUR BREATH AWAY…
Half way up the hill, take a well-earned rest to view the panorama. You can clearly see the three spring-line villages: Edburton in front of you, Fulking to the right and Poynings beyond.

thyme

forced them to the less-hospitable downs. You can still make out the ancient terraces formed by ploughing. The village was probably abandoned after the Black Death (bubonic plague) had wiped out much of Britain's population. Once again, the downs became the exclusive domain of sheep.

Find the lost village
On the right is the site of the deserted Medieval village of Perching. People moved here in the 13th century, when over-population

☞ *Over the brow, head towards higher gate, then follow path back to the Devil's Dyke.*

Countryside Kids

From another planet!
☻ This walk takes you across strange bumpy places called bostals. They are like craters on the moon and some weird-looking plants grow in them:

☻ Yellow-wort has flowers like yellow stars, and leaves which appear to have been speared by its long grey stem.

☻ Even stranger is carline thistle – it has golden yellow spiky flowers, but always appears to be dead! It was once known as "boar's throat" – can you see any resemblance to a hairy boar?

carline thistle

yellow-wort

Continuing the grazing tradition

Without sheep grazing, the grassland is quickly invaded by thorn bushes, shading out the rich wildlife of the downs. The National Trust is continuing the grazing tradition to protect the wildlife of the downs, particularly the unusual flowers. Bushes which have taken hold are being removed to restore the ancient landscape.

☞ About this walk...

Distance: 3½ miles (allow 2½ hours)

Terrain: Steep climb up scarp slope. Muddy in winter. Several stiles

Start: The Devil's Dyke pub, signposted off A27, 6 miles N of Hove

Public Transport: No. 77 bus to Devil's Dyke. Visit www.buses.co.uk or phone 01273 292480

Facilities: Devil's Dyke Hotel, Shepherd & Dog pub

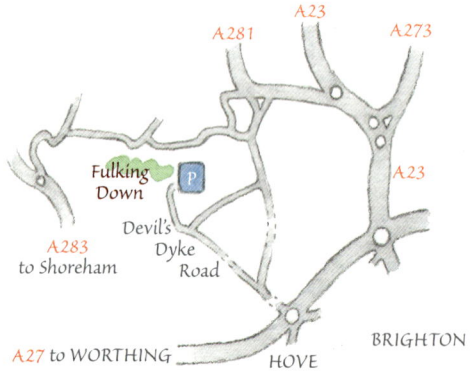

Welcome to Black Cap

☞ *Cross road from lay-by, go through gate and straight up right-hand track.*

FLOWERS LINE THE WAY
The sunken track you follow is a 'bostal', etched by the footsteps of countless sheep (see Fulking Down walk). In spring and summer, its sides are smothered with wild flowers. Keen eyes might spot the aptly-named bee and frog orchids, or musk orchids that look like tiny Christmas trees.

bee orchid

☞ *Pass two junctions, continuing up to top of hill.*

MARCH TO VICTORY
It is said that Simon de Montfort's army followed this route in 1264, marching over the hill to clash with King Henry III's men in the Battle of Lewes. The King was defeated, and a treaty known as the Mise of Lewes was signed.

☞ *At top, the bostal leads into open downland.*

A SACRED PLACE
This isolated, breathtaking spot has been cherished since ancient times. The mounds on the left at the top of the bostal are burial places, dating back to the Bronze Age and Saxon period.

☞ *Turn left and follow path to viewpoint on ridge.*

DOWNLAND PANORAMA
At the viewpoint, the scarp slope plummets down in front of you to meet the flat plain of the Weald. Turning towards the coast, Brighton lies straight ahead, with Newhaven to the left. Some people believe that the name 'Black Cap' originates from the plantation which resembles a black cap on the hilltop; others suggest it is named after a nearby windmill.

☞ *Continue down hill, taking track to right of the crest. (For short walk, take left-hand track to waymark post, then follow left-hand path down steep slope to bostal.)*

SCRUB BASHING
The scrub you pass on the left provides important food and shelter for birds and butterflies. But its growth needs to be controlled or it will smother the open grassland. 'Scrub bashing' involves clearing young trees and bushes, but leaving some sheltered thickets as wildlife habitats. The reddish-brown Sussex cattle which graze the down help by eating the shoots of new trees.

START

☞ Turn right at waymark sign about 100 metres after bridle-gate. Follow path down into a valley, turning right where it meets the main track. Follow straight on along shady track.

WILDLIFE IN THE WOODS

You now enter a more secluded world from the open downs, peaceful yet rich in wildlife. Small, sunny glades are blanketed with yellow rock rose and the purple of devil's bit scabious; while red campion and rosebay willowherb form pink borders along the paths. At dusk in summer, the air is perfumed with the sweet scent of honeysuckle. If you are quiet, you might spot badgers, foxes and roe deer.

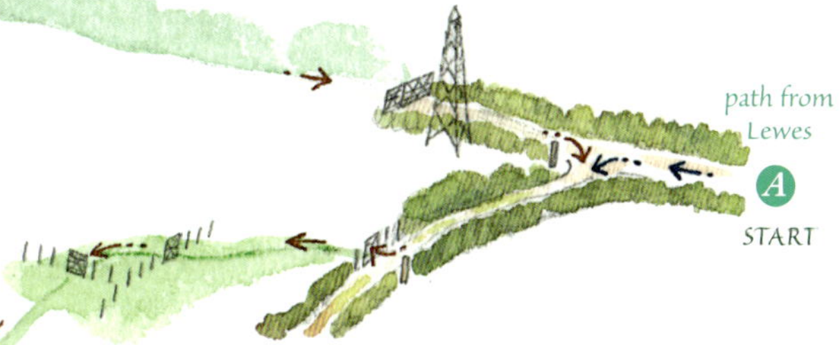

short walk back

short walk or continue

path from Lewes

A START

☞ Cross the bracken coombe, and take the left-hand fork under the power lines, waymarked with a blue arrow. Follow main track continuing straight ahead.

TREES TO NOTE

The twisted, multi-stemmed trees along the path are hazels, last coppiced up to 40 years ago (see Drovers walk). Look out for an old buckthorn tree on the right, especially attractive in autumn with its hanging yellow leaves and dark purple berries. Further on you pass two large ash trees on the left, thought to mark a medieval boundary.

buckthorn

☞ Continue through gate by pylon, then turn right along woodland path. **A** *(Alternative start from Lewes.)* Turn right at bridle-gate and cut diagonally across field to another gate. Go down hill to far bottom corner of field and through bridle-gate.

EVER-CHANGING COLOURS

As you walk down the field, look right to see the myriad colours of Ashcombe Bottom; green and yellow, turning to russet, red and gold in the autumn. The walk takes you through the heart of this peaceful woodland. Please note that signs might ask you to stay on the paths when the pheasant shoot is taking place (October to February).

☞ Stay on main track which becomes steep and narrow. Go through gate at top, then straight on up field. Retrace your steps back from the top of the bostal. (If you started at Lewes, turn right and head for viewpoint.)

Countryside Kids

WILDLIFE DETECTIVES!
Use your skills to track down the wildlife of Ashcombe Bottom:

🙂 Badgers leave large four-toed claw prints in the mud, as well as distinct pathways and tunnels in the undergrowth.

🙂 Foxes leave footprints like a dog but with longer claws, and have a strong musty smell which lingers for up to an hour.

badger   fox

🙂 Inspect the nuts under the hazel trees to discover who has been to dinner! Mice nibble away, leaving lots of tiny teeth marks in the nut. Dormice carve small neat holes, while squirrels just crack the nut wide open!

LIGHT IN THE WOODS

Don't be alarmed if you see some trees being cut down in Ashcombe Bottom. Small open glades are being created to allow sunlight to penetrate the trees, and so encourage downland flowers to grow. This in turn attracts a wealth of butterflies, insects and birds. Likewise, the edges of the rides (tracks) are cleared to create corridors of light throughout the woods.

☞ About this walk...

DISTANCE: 4½ miles (allow up to 3 hours). Or short walk of 1 hour

TERRAIN: Steep climb to and from summit. Otherwise easy underfoot

START: Lay-by on B2116 (limited parking – four cars maximum), off A275, 3 miles NE of Lewes

Ⓐ **ALTERNATIVE START FROM LEWES:** 1½ miles from Lewes Prison crossroads. See map

PUBLIC TRANSPORT: For buses or trains to Lewes call Traveline on 0871 200 22 33 or visit www.traveline.org.uk

FACILITIES: None on walk

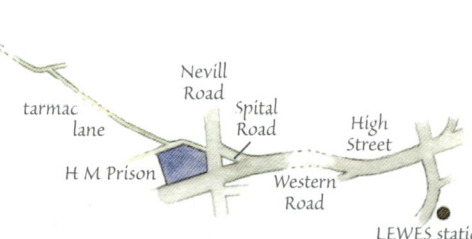

National Trust

Cuckmere Valley

Follow the Cuckmere River as it snakes down to the sea, where bird cries haunt the air, and days end in shimmering pink-gold sunsets

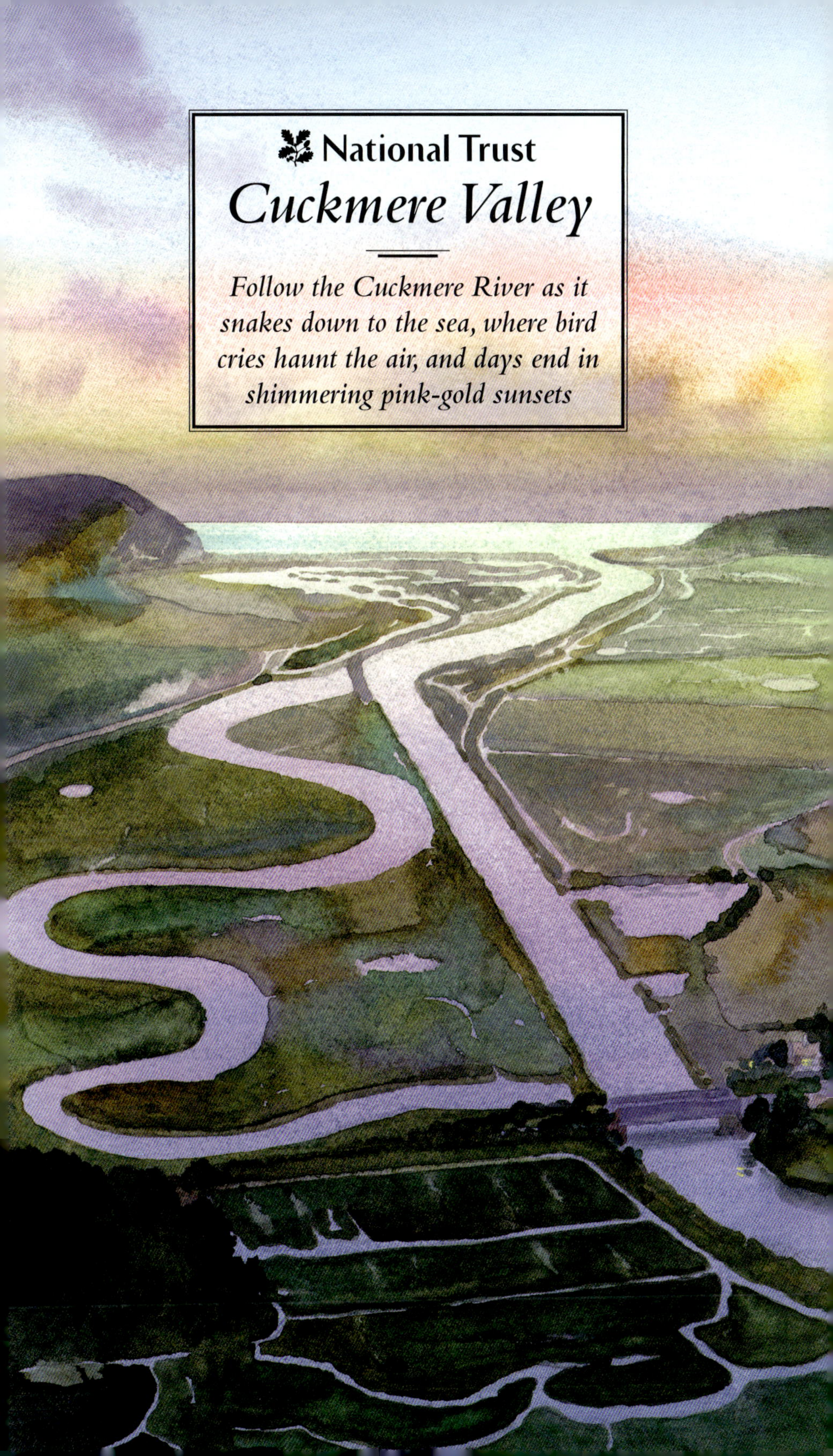

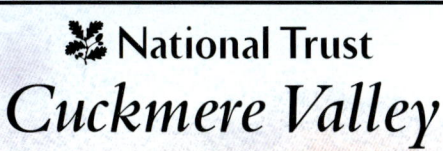

Welcome to Cuckmere Valley

The two walks take in different sections of the river, and can be joined to make one long walk. The river is tidal and extremely fast flowing – the name Cuckmere is derived from 'quick mere'. While by the water, please ensure that children stay on the paths.

WALK 1 Frog Firle Farm

☞ *Take footpath furthest from entrance of car park and follow track to left, through kissing gate and down hill.*

ANCIENT FEATURES
The mound you pass on the left is a Bronze Age barrow (burial place). The sunken track ahead was the main transport route, before the current road was built. As you walk down, the chalk figure of the Litlington White Horse becomes visible on the right. It was originally cut in 1836 by the tenant of Frog Firle Farm, and is now maintained by the National Trust.

☞ *Continue down, go through bridle-gate at bottom of hill, and follow track towards Litlington bridge.*

HISTORIC FARMS
Take a look over the brow on your left to see Tile Barn Farm. The barn dates back to 1800, but was burnt down in an arson attack in 1834. The ponds and reed beds were restored in 1998 and 2008 by the National Trust to provide wildlife habitats and an education facility for schools.

Notice the uneven ground at the bottom of the hill – thought to be the remains of a medieval farmstead.

☞ *Beyond the medieval remains, climb river bank. Turn left over stile and go along river to bridge.*

Frogs and toads

On the hill to your left is Frog Firle farmhouse, now a Youth Hostel. The reason for the name 'frog' is unknown, but 'firle' is thought to be a Roman word for the 'wild lands' outside a Roman estate. In spring, toads appear here in droves, migrating from the downs to the ditches. Local people form 'toad patrols' to help them cross the road!

☞ *Cross the bridge, turn sharp right before waymark post, and follow river. (For refreshments at Litlington, cross bridge and turn left. Take next right to village – a five minute walk.)*

Tales of the riverbank

Listen for the sudden splashes of fish rising for food, especially large grey mullet. You are likely to see swans and herons here, as well as tiny shy coots, speeding away with their white heads bobbing (hence the saying 'bald as a coot'). If you are lucky, you might even spot the brilliant blue flash of a kingfisher.

☞ *Cross stile and continue, walking under the white horse. At waymark, turn right and climb steps. (To extend your walk to Chyngton Farm, continue along path to river, then follow river path to the Golden Galleon pub.) Go through kissing gate, up steps and along gravel path to car park.*

WALK 2
Chyngton Farm

☞ *From South Hill Barn car park, follow centre track straight down hill.*

DRAGONFLY AIR-SHOW
In summer, look out for dragonflies in the ditches by the river bank. Dragonflies fall into two categories – darters and hawkers. Hawkers patrol up and down stalking prey, while darters rest at the water's edge, before dashing out to snatch their prey mid-air. If you are lucky you might spot the iridescent green and blue of an emperor, Britain's largest dragonfly. Damselflies are smaller and more delicate.

☞ *Go over next stile and continue to bridge. Cross bridge, turn left and follow base of hill. (If you are weary, turn right and re-trace your steps back up the hill.)*

RED STAR THISTLE
In summer, this part of the valley is covered with the light green leaves and pinky-red flowers of red star thistle. Yet this plant is extremely rare nationally. Notice the spiky flowers of teasels – which were once used to prepare fleeces for spinning.

SCRUB FULL OF FLOWERS
There is colour here year-round. In early spring, blackthorn is covered in a flurry of white flowers. Next comes the pink explosion of hawthorn and brambles, and the sweet-scented white blooms of elder. Fruits add the autumnal hues; bluey-black sloes, deep purple elder berries and scarlet haws. The yellow, coconut-scented flowers of gorse brighten-up all the seasons.

...AND BIRDS
Thanks to the endless supply of nectar and berries, the scrub is alive with birds. Yellowhammers, goldfinches and chaffinches add more dashes of colour, while dark metallic-blue swallows dip and dive, their tail feathers streaming in the wind. Slate-grey peregrine falcons hide in the sun, waiting to snatch smaller birds in flight.

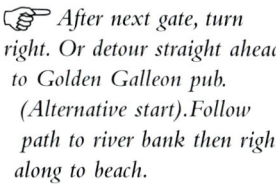

☞ *After cattle grid, turn left over stile and bear left along scrub line.*

BATTLE OF THE TIDES
The flood-plain below is a mixture of both natural and man-made features. The river meanders were cut off in 1846 to form a canal. The straight drainage ditches were dug by farmers to improve the pasture for cattle grazing. At the river mouth is a shingle bank, created to prevent flooding of low-lying fields.

☞ *After the hump, drop down field heading for stile at bottom.*

CLOUDS OF BUTTERFLIES
As you cross this field in summer, butterflies will rise all around you. Look out for skippers, meadow browns, blues and red admirals.

☞ *Go over stile and turn left. Go along footpath, through gate and straight on.*

WILDLIFE ON THE WING
In winter, you can see a huge variety of birds feeding on the marsh. Look out for little egrets – pure white elegant birds, like herons but smaller.

In summer the most dramatic air-borne activity comes from brilliantly-coloured dragonflies and damselflies.

☞ *After next gate, turn right. Or detour straight ahead to Golden Galleon pub. (Alternative start). Follow path to river bank then right along to beach.*

ANCIENT SETTLEMENT
The medieval village of Exceat once stood across the valley. With rich grazing land, bountiful fishing and waterways for transport, it was an ideal location. However, the village was almost wiped out in the 14th century by the 'Black Death' (bubonic plague).

LIFE IN STRANGE PLACES
Notice the unusual plants on the marshes which have adapted to survive the toughest conditions – salt, twice daily flooding and biting winds. Sea purslane coats the banks with soft, silver-green leaves, while glasswort shimmers like red and green glass cacti. In the even less hospitable shingle by the beach, yellow horned poppies thrive, together with sea kale – you can't miss its huge frilly purple leaves.

☞ *Go through gate onto beach, walk along shingle bank, through gate and past coastguard cottages. The track leads back to car park. (If you started at the Golden Galleon pub, now follow directions from cattle grid just after start.)*

THE SEVEN SISTERS
As you walk up the hill, pause to look back over the spectacular view of the Seven Sisters. The lighthouse in the distance is Belle Tout at Birling Gap (see Seven Sisters leaflet).

Walk 1 – Frog Firle Farm

Distance: 3 miles (allow 2½ hours)

Terrain: One extremely steep hill, otherwise flat along river. Very muddy at times

Start: High and Over car park (not NT) on Alfriston Road between Seaford and Alfriston, 3 miles N of Seaford

Facilities: Detour to Litlington village

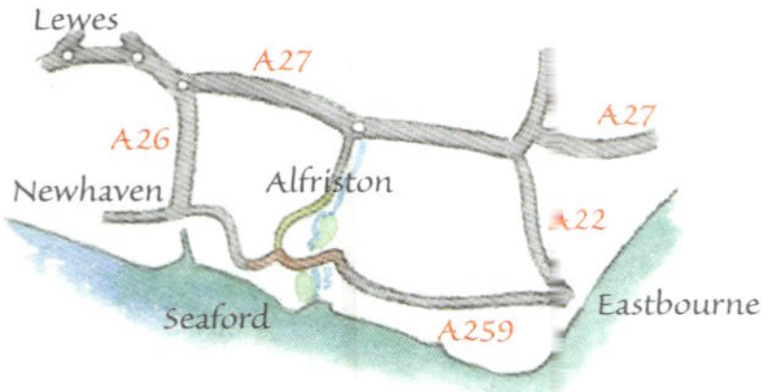

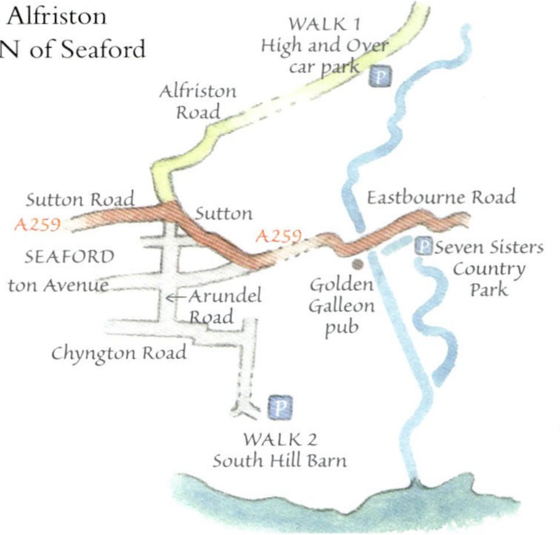

Walk 2 – Chyngton Farm

Distance: 3 miles (allow 2 hours)

Terrain: Easy walk, mostly flat. Pushchair accessible (see detour on map)

Start: South Hill Barn car park (not NT), off A259 (Seaford to Eastbourne road). See map

Alternative Start: Park at Seven Sisters Country Park (fee – not NT), off A259, 1½ miles E of Seaford

Facilities: Golden Galleon pub, Seven Sisters Country Park

Public Transport: For bus information call Traveline on 0871 200 22 33 or visit www.traveline.org.uk

Please note: This walk passes over Lewes District Council land and Seaford Local Nature Reserve

Countryside Kids

WATCH OUT – LOW FLYING WILDLIFE!

🙂 In spring, young dragonflies emerge from husks and dry their colourful wings in the sun. See if you can spot the empty husks left on the waterside plants.

🙂 Watch out for mid-air collisions as male dragonflies battle for territory in summer.

🙂 If you hear a loud laughing noise in the air, it is probably a redshank, one of the noisiest birds here. Watch out for the white stripe on its wing as it flashes past.

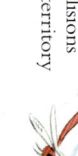

National Trust
The Seven Sisters

Where the flower-embroidered downs plunge into the sea in a dazzling wall of white

Welcome to the Seven Sisters

Walk 1 *Crowlink*

Why Seven Sisters?
From Birling Gap, you get a breathtaking panorama of the Seven Sisters stretching to Cuckmere Haven, with Seaford Head beyond. This area was first recorded in the 15th century as the Seven Cliffs. As for the origin of the term 'sisters' – your guess is as good as ours! The brilliant white of the cliffs is due to constant erosion by the sea.

☞ *From Birling Gap, follow track up hill on right (behind toilets), through gate, then left at yellow waymarking sign. Go through gate and up onto the down.*

A treat for the senses
Cucumber-scented salad burnett, a nationally rare plant, thrives in the turf here. On warm days the air is sweet with the coconut aroma of gorse. Listen for skylarks, rising from the grass to fill the air with melodious song; while in the coombes, watch for the dashing eye stripes and bobbing white rumps of wheatears. In summer, clouds of butterflies rise from the grass.

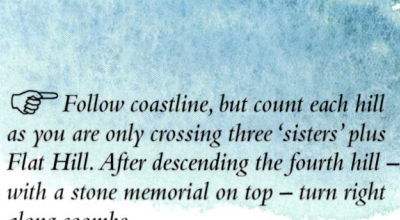
dew pond

Flat Hill

skylark

salad burnett

☞ *Follow coastline, but count each hill as you are only crossing three 'sisters' plus Flat Hill. After descending the fourth hill – with a stone memorial on top – turn right along coombe.*

Cottages lost to the sea
Before you turn inland, notice the markings on the base of the hill ahead. These are the foundations of coastguard cottages, which became unsafe due to cliff erosion and were subsequently used for artillery target practice in World War Two.

Activity in the air
During World War Two, the tranquillity here was often shattered by fighter planes, zooming in from the sea to land at a nearby airfield. The unusual stone building on the hillside opposite housed the pilots. For airborne drama these days, visit the dew pond beside the path – where colourful dragonflies and damselflies stage spectacular summer flying shows.

☞ *Pass pond, then bear right along path to gate, then straight on.*

☞ *Go through far gate and down through meadow.*

WHERE THE WIND BLOWS
As you climb, notice the trees to your left, sculpted by the prevailing winds to look like hunched old men.

☞ *Go through Crowlink car park* **A** *(alternative start point). Walk along track towards main road, then turn right through gate into Friston Churchyard.*

WASHED ASHORE
Look out for the simple graves of unknown persons who were 'washed ashore'. Some date back to 1830.

A FIELD FULL OF FLOWERS

This lovely hay meadow is known as Hobb's Eares. In Sussex dialect, 'eares' means arable land, and Hobbs would have been the surname of the owner. In spring, the meadow is a sea of white and yellow daisies and buttercups; while in summer, a wave of deep purple and gold washes over as knapweed appears through the drying grass.

☞ *Near bottom, veer right and pick up path through trees. (Gate at bottom of Hobb's Eares takes you to East Dean village and the historic Tiger Inn.) At top, turn right and climb hill.*

early spider orchid

ARACHNAPHOBES BEWARE!

Watch where you tread in early spring. The hillside is a site for the rare early spider orchid, its flowers looking every bit like black furry bodies.

☞ *Go over steps set in wall and head up slope to gate. (If gate area is too wet, detour to kissing gate shown on map, then walk back along fence to join walk again.)*

ALARMING CALL

If you hear a loud laughing call from the trees to your left, you have probably disturbed a green woodpecker. It has brilliant green and yellow feathers, and a red crown – but all you are likely to see is its yellow rump as it swoops away from you.

☞ *Go through gate and skirt round left of field. Pass another gate, then go through the next, crossing field to red barn. In front of barn, pick up sunken track over hill, and follow to gate, where you meet track to Birling Gap.*

WALK 2 *Birling Gap*

☞ *Walk up steps behind coastguard cottages and straight up onto the down.*

ON THE LOOK-OUT

For centuries, customs officers have kept vigil along these cliffs, while smugglers lurked on the beaches below. There have been cottages here since the 1820s to house the families of the coastguards who worked from Birling Gap. Notice the mossy patch at the cliff top, the site of a look-out tower which was demolished in 1991.

AMAZING TECHNICOLOUR TURF

The downs are sprinkled with flowers all year, but the most spectacular display is in summer, when viper's bugloss and weld adorn the turf in the most intense blue and yellow. The name viper's bugloss dates back to when the plant was used as a cure for snake-bite. In autumn, clumps of heather, a rarity on chalk downland, turn to vibrant purple.

weld

viper's bugloss

👉 Turn left at path towards small wood.

WOODLAND WILDLIFE
The cool, dappled shade of Horseshoe Plantation supports different wildlife to the sunny, open downs. Speckled wood butterflies dance in shafts of sunlight, and families of tits chatter amidst the branches.
See if you can spot the strange flowers of yellow rattle, resembling hooked witches' noses. When ripe, the seeds rattle in their pods, once said to be the herald of hay-making time.

👉 At top, head towards the lighthouse, either along the cliff path or through the scrub.

SCRUB SAFARI
Walk quietly through the scrub for a wildlife extravaganza. The flowers of hawthorn, blackthorn and gorse provide a year-round larder for insects, in turn feeding a host of birds. Dapper little stonechats keep watch from the highest branches, while kestrels hover menacingly before dropping down to snatch their prey. Common lizards dash across the path, and you might spot an adder basking in the sun.

👉 Follow path to left of lighthouse. Beyond, a detour to cliff top gives splendid views of Beachy Head. Drop down and skirt round the scrub to meet path. (Pushchair users follow lighthouse track down).

LIGHTHOUSE ON THE MOVE
The lighthouse, Belle Tout, was moved inland in March 1999 to escape the receding coastline. It was originally built in the 1820s, but became a private home after being replaced by Beachy Head lighthouse. In January 1999, a 45 metre deep landslide occurred at Beachy Head, the largest recorded this century.

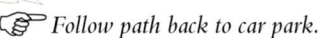

👉 Follow path back to car park.

ANCIENT SETTLEMENTS
As you leave the wood, look up to your left and you can see a mound running along the down. This is the remains of an ancient rampart which would have encircled the entire hill. Birling Gap itself is named after the 'Baerelingas', a group of Anglo Saxons who settled here in AD 489.

Countryside Kids

NATURE'S NASTY HABITS

🙂 In the valleys, look out for bumbling bloody-nosed beetles. Their trick is to spit out a red drop of horrible-tasting liquid if threatened.

🙂 Don't get too close to fulmars on the cliffs they might dive-bomb you, and spit a foul-smelling liquid through their peculiar nose tubes.

🙂 In summer you might spot tall yellow ragwort flowers in the fields. Bees and moths love its nectar, but it is called 'stinking Billy' in Scotland due to its unpleasant smell when bruised. Ragwort can be poisonous to sheep and horses.

PROTECTING THE DOWNLAND WILDLIFE

The varied wildlife of the downs is due to the mosaic of different habitats. Without careful management by the National Trust many species could be lost. Grazing by sheep or cattle keeps the turf short, crucial to the survival of many downland flowers. Patches of scrub provide shelter for birds, but must be cut back on rotation to prevent them from smothering the grassland.

☞ About these walks...

DISTANCE:
Walk 1: 4½ miles (allow 3½ hours)
Walk 2: 1½ miles (allow up to 1 hour)

TERRAIN:
Walk 1: Very hilly. Muddy in places. Several stiles.
Walk 2: Easy walk. Moderate slopes. Pushchair accessible (with slight detour)

START:
Birling Gap or Crowlink (A) (alternative start for Walk 1) car parks, off A259, 18 miles E of Brighton

PUBLIC TRANSPORT:
Daily buses to Birling Gap or Friston (for Crowlink car park). For details call Traveline on 0871 200 22 33 or visit www.traveline.org.uk

FACILITIES:
Toilets, café and restaurant at Birling Gap. Walk 1 passes the Tiger Inn, East Dean

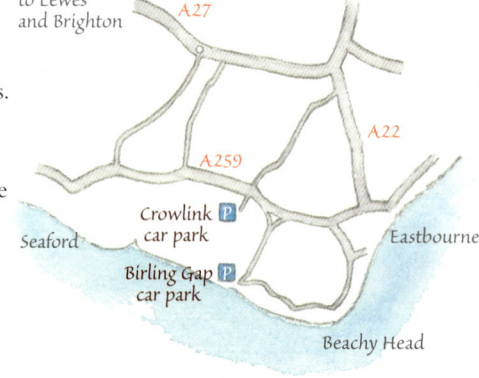

Please note: Walk 2 crosses Eastbourne Borough Council land.